NATURE ACTIVITY BOOK
for little ones

NATURE
ACTIVITY BOOK
for little ones

100+ ACTIVITIES for EVERYDAY OUTDOOR FUN

SAMANTHA LEWIS

Illustrated by Rotem Teplow

A Brightly Book

Z KIDS · NEW YORK

Copyright © 2022 by Penguin Random House LLC

Published in the United States by Z Kids, an imprint of Zeitgeist™ a division of Penguin Random House LLC, New York.
penguinrandomhouse.com

Zeitgeist™ is a trademark of Penguin Random House LLC

ISBN: 9780593435441
Ebook ISBN: 9780593435588

Author photo by Torrie Hazelwood
Illustrations by Rotem Teplow
Book design by Katy Brown

Printed in the United States of America

1 3 5 7 9 10 8 6 4 2

First Edition

To everyone who steps outside

Contents

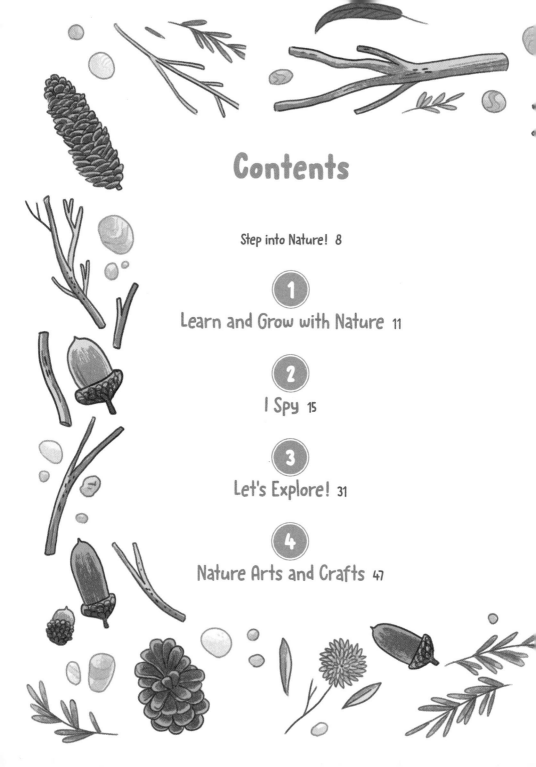

Step into Nature!

Everyone has a favorite spot. A place where they feel comfortable, a space to think, a place all their own. For many, that space is in nature, with its sounds, smells, and sense of freedom and the chance to move. The place where we can learn about ourselves.

But grown-ups aren't the only ones who benefit from the great outdoors. Children also reap the rewards of nature—calmness, curiosity, connectivity, and empathy—starting at a young age. I have had the chance to witness this firsthand from Colorado to China. Through my time working in outdoor education, I have seen the good that being outdoors can do for kids. Whether it's breathing in the fresh air, stretching their legs, or developing social-emotional skills, every child deserves the chance to experience nature's benefits.

The ability to understand the world around us begins at a very early age. Bringing a young child outdoors instills a sense of curiosity and wonder, teaches problem-solving and effective communication, and helps develop a sense of responsibility. These benefits don't stop with school readiness; they translate into skills your child will carry through life.

Each child is different and will profit differently from their time outside. But most important, parents and children should spend the time outside together. I say "parent" as a shorthand for all guardians, grandparents, siblings, or other caregivers. It doesn't matter what role you play in the child's life; what matters is the connection you create by spending time together. Sharing that time together outdoors deepens your bond and creates a lifelong relationship with one another and the greater world.

This book will show you creative ways to grow your child's relationship with nature and discover its joys. The activities in these pages require few materials (and those that are necessary are inexpensive items you can find around your home). In addition, you won't have to spend a lot of time preparing for these activities; most require little more than reading the instructions and stepping outside to experience the joy of nature. And the activities are designated by level of difficulty: one leaf for easy, two leaves for medium, and three leaves for challenging. If a particular activity or part of an activity is too challenging for a younger child, feel free to adapt it to fit your child's age level and abilities.

Finally, always keep safety in mind. Remember: no touching or chasing animals; stay away from poison ivy and the like; be careful around water; watch the weather; dress appropriately for the season; wear sunscreen or protective clothing; use bug spray; hydrate; wear sturdy, comfortable footwear; and take plenty of breaks.

With this book you will embark on a journey of growth together, whether through developmental milestones, bonding, or learning skills for a lifetime. The first steps of this journey stretch beyond the pages of this book, to the hiking trails, mountains, fields, beaches, and forests you and your child explore. Have fun on your journey together!

1

Learn and Grow with Nature

It's not hard to see how tall a tree has grown, to look up and notice how the branches touch the sky—but what you don't see are the roots, the way they intertwine, digging ever deeper into the ground to get more nutrients out of the soil. Humans are the same. You can see our bodies but not how we develop and grow. Our limbs can reach to the sky, too, and our roots also look for nutrients. According to the Centers for Disease Control and Prevention (CDC), child growth and development—their roots—can be placed into four categories: movement and physical development, cognitive development, communication and language development, and social-emotional development. Spending time outdoors helps develop all these characteristics, sometimes in surprising ways.

When people think of the outdoors they mostly think of physical movement and, through that, physical development. Children can work on their physical development by walking, running, climbing, and even just holding on to objects. Nature allows children to walk over uneven ground, helping them develop a skill they would not be able to indoors. Holding a stick and hitting it against a rock helps them strengthen the muscles in their hands that they will use to hold a pencil when they're ready for school, ultimately helping them develop their handwriting skills.

Cognitive development is all about how we think, perceive, reason, and remember the world around us. This is the area of development where your child develops their information processing, language, memory, and reasoning skills. Many children learn how to process the world they are experiencing through play. Allowing your child to play outdoors helps them learn about other people and the world, and work on reasoning and information-processing skills. Learning the names of plants and animals helps with their language skills and memory. The world is a big place, and there's a lot to learn!

Communication and language are so much more than talking to one another. They are how humans interact and understand meaning. Nothing a human does that involves another human can be successful without effective communication. Going outdoors to develop communication and language skills doesn't always look like going outside and talking to trees. Most of the time, going outdoors is not an individual activity. You go on hikes together, play games together, swim in the ocean together. The outdoors is a space where you need to talk in order to move forward. You discuss which trail to take, ask questions about the trees, and talk about what you brought with you. According to the CDC, two-year-olds should be able to follow simple instructions and five-year-olds should be able to tell a simple story using full sentences. Spending time outdoors together helps your child learn these skills and hit important developmental milestones.

One of the things I love about learning is that it never ends. This is especially true for social-emotional learning. Social-emotional learning is the area where we learn to create and retain positive relationships, make responsible decisions, gain the skills to recognize and manage emotions, and so much more. The CDC lists many milestones for social-emotional learning, including the ability to play alongside other children at age two, and beginning to play *with* other children as well, including games of chase. The CDC says five-year-olds are more likely to argue with rules—an important part of social-emotional learning. Some aspects of social-emotional learning, like testing boundaries, may give parents a headache, but they are important parts of child development.

Learning these skills in the outdoors allows for freedom to learn. Nature is a physical space designed for running, jumping, observing, reasoning, communicating, managing emotions, and pushing boundaries. It is a space that allows children to develop skills in a place that gives them a deeper understanding of the greater world and gets them excited about what's around them. It's an inspiring opportunity to see the world far beyond the four walls we live in.

② I Spy

There's so much to see in nature! Some of it is big and bright; some of it is quiet and humble. But you can't see any of it if you don't look. This group of activities will help your child sharpen their observational skills, see nature with new eyes, and focus on what they see. They will notice the beauty that is out there and develop a deeper understanding of what nature has to offer.

COLORS OF NATURE

The natural world is full of beauty and colors. How many colors does your child see? Have them match the colors of the rainbow to the great variety of colors in nature.

 EASY

What You'll Need

Paper

Crayons, colored pencils, pens, or markers

1. Help your child draw a rainbow on a piece of paper.

2. Go outside together and have them choose a color in the rainbow and then look for something in nature that matches that color. Do this for all the colors of the rainbow.

3. Talk about how many colors are in the rainbow. How many colors did your child see in nature?

4. Talk about the colors they haven't found. Can the two of you think of a time—perhaps a different season—when you might be able to see those colors?

BONUS ACTIVITY!

Look at a leaf together and talk about the shapes your child can find in it. Do they see triangles? Squares? Anything else?

A PLACE OF YOUR OWN

Make the great outdoors a little bit smaller and more accessible for your child by creating their very own space. Work together to find a place they can return to time and time again. Help them use this place to observe nature over days, weeks, months, and seasons to see how their place changes. Giving a child a sense of ownership over a space in nature encourages them to feel more confident outdoors.

EASY

What You'll Need

A nearby outdoor area that is both accessible and comfortable

1. Together, choose an outdoor space that your child can return to again and again. It can be at a park, on a playground, in a wooded area, or on the top of a hill. Choose somewhere close to home that you both like.

2. Help your child find a spot in that outdoor space that they can call their own. It can be a bench, a swing, or a patch of grass.

3. Let your child give this spot a name.

4. Return to this spot as often as possible. Always call the spot by its name. For example, you can say, "After lunch we are going to go to your bench garden to read" or "Would you like to go to The Hill this afternoon?"

5. Pick out three objects in nature that may change with time (like a tree, a flower, and a bush). Talk about the changes your child sees in these three objects every time you visit their spot.

SIGN OF THE TIMES

At different times of the year one spot can look very different. What can your child find that proves the seasons are changing?

 EASY

What You'll Need

Paper

Pen or pencil

1. Sit down together outside and make a list of all the things that you and your child can think of that mean the seasons are changing.

2. Walk around with the list, looking for the items on it.

3. Collect these items with your child. What can you find other than leaves? What colors indicate changing seasons?

4. Have your child count how many seasonal objects they can collect. Is one object easier to find than others?

BONUS ACTIVITY!

Have your child point out an animal they see regularly. Ask them where they think that animal lives. Is it in a nest? A tunnel underground? A bush?

SHAPES OF THE FOREST

Have you ever noticed how a tree can look like a triangle and a bush can look like a circle? Can your child spot the shapes in nature?

 EASY

What You'll Need

Paper

Crayons, colored pencils, pens, or markers

1. Look at a tree with your child and ask them to draw what shape they see.

2. If the tree is more than one shape, ask your child to identify and count the number of shapes.

3. Walk around together and identify other shapes in flowers, bushes, and different kinds of trees.

WHAT'S THE WEATHER UP THERE?

Help your child work on their observational skills every day. Nature doesn't have to be deep in the woods or high up in the mountains. While walking to school, playing in the backyard, or taking a hike, ask your child questions about what they see. As an added benefit, repetition helps children learn and create new habits of observation.

EASY

What You'll Need

A sheet of paper

A pen or pencil

BONUS ACTIVITY!

Ask your child if they think they can predict the weather. What do they think the weather will be like later today? What do they see or hear that makes them think that?

1. Ask your child questions about what they see:

   * *What color is the sky?*
   * *Are there a lot of clouds in the sky?*
   * *How many trees do you see?*

2. Ask them about what they feel:

   * *Is it warm or cold out?*
   * *Do you feel the sun on your skin?*
   * *Can you feel the wind?*

3. When you return home, record the weather your child has observed on a sheet of paper. Keep track of the weather for seven days and talk about what the weather was like for the week.

WHAT DO YOU SEE?

Nature is everywhere! Even when you aren't looking, you can find it. Play a game of I Spy with your child both inside and outside, and then compare the results. You may be surprised by how much the two of you see!

EASY

What You'll Need

Paper

Pen or pencil

1. Starting inside, write down all the natural elements you and your child can see outside your window under the header "Inside."

2. Go outside and add a new header on the paper called "Outside."

3. Under that, write all the natural elements you and your child can see right outside your door.

4. Ask your child what new objects in nature they see as they step farther away from your door, and record them on the paper. How does this column compare to the "Inside" column?

5. Ask your child if they think the list will get longer the farther they walk, and why.

COMPLIMENT A TREE

Making observations at a young age sets up your child for school preparedness and a lifetime of curiosity. Talking to inanimate objects helps children relieve the stress of talking to adults and others they may not know.

EASY

What You'll Need

A tree

1. Find a tree your child likes.

2. Take some time and look at the tree together. Walk around it, touch it, and ask your child:

   * *Does the tree feel bumpy or smooth?*
   * *Can you see any bugs in the tree?*
   * *Do you hear any animals in the tree?*
   * *Does the tree have a smell?*

3. Help your child tell the tree what they like about it.

IS ANYONE HOME?

Habitats are the natural types of homes or environments an animal can live in. The five main habitats are grassland, desert, forest, polar region, and aquatic. You and your child can discover what habitat you reside in, even if you live in an urban or suburban area. Do you see squirrels and birds, or do you live near a body of water? Using a piece of paper and an internet connection (to research which animals live where), can you and your child figure out what type of habitat you are surrounded by?

 MEDIUM

What You'll Need

Paper

Pen or pencil

1. Take a walk together and write down the different animals you see.

2. Ask your child if the animals share any characteristics:

    * *Which ones have fur?*
    * *Do any have flippers or fins?*
    * *Do some have feathers?*

3. Write down the animals' characteristics and work together to figure out which type of habitat you live in.

WHO GOES THERE?

Children have an easier time understanding the world around them when they can identify themselves in it. By seeing their footprints in the ground they will understand how animals leave prints of their own.

EASY

What You'll Need

Mud, sand, dirt, or snow

An empty spot on the ground

1. Find a muddy, sandy, dirt-filled, or snowy space big enough for the two of you.

2. Stand next to each other, shoulder to shoulder.

3. Step away from the space together. Look back where you were standing and compare your footprints.

4. Ask your child:

   * *What do you see?*
   * *What shapes are on the bottom of your shoes?*
   * *Is my shoe print bigger or smaller than yours?*
   * *Why do you think we left footprints on the ground?*

EVERYONE POOPS!

The easiest way to discover if animals are around is by finding their poop. Animal droppings come in all shapes and sizes. Help your child hone their observational skills by asking lots of questions about the droppings. It's always fun to talk about poop!

 EASY

What You'll Need

Animal droppings

1. Look at animal droppings you've found together (without getting too close) and ask your child:

   * What shape are they?
   * What colors are they?
   * Are they dry or moist?
   * If they're dry, do you think they've been here a long time or a short time?
   * Is the pile of droppings big or small?
   * Are the droppings themselves big or small?

2. Based on their answers, can your child guess what type of animal might have left those droppings behind?

MAP IT OUT

Maps help us stay on course, but sometimes what's on the paper and what's in the world are different. Maybe the map shows trees on the left side of the trail, but you and your child don't see those trees. Or maybe a tree has fallen onto the trail. Can your child spot the differences?

 MEDIUM

What You'll Need

A map of a local hiking trail or somewhere you and your child like to explore

Crayons, colored pencils, pens, or markers

1. Go on a hike together with a map!

2. Ask your child to draw trees and rocks and other objects on the map when they're not represented.

3. Help your child create their own landmarks and mark them on the map.

ONE TREE, FOUR SEASONS

The seasons change the way the world looks. Pick one object with your child—in this case, a tree—to see how the seasons are changing.

 MEDIUM

What You'll Need

Paper

Crayons, colored pencils, pens, or markers

A tree close to home

1. Ask your child to choose a tree that you both see daily. Maybe it's on your way to school or in a nearby park.

2. Together, visit the tree monthly to see if it has changed.

3. Have your child draw the tree in the different seasons and describe how it has changed.

(3)

Let's Explore!

Children learn by observing, but sometimes that's only the first step into nature. Just as explorers experience more by climbing the highest peaks, sending probes to the deepest underwater trenches, and flying among the stars, your child can learn more by stepping out of their comfort zone and experiencing the world around them. Use the activities in this chapter to help your child interact with and learn from nature.

YOU CHOOSE THE WAY

So many kids have little say in their own lives. They don't get to decide when they go to bed or school. Adding autonomy to a routine or short amount of time can help them develop an independent spirit. Show confidence in your child by letting them take charge of your exploration.

 MEDIUM

What You'll Need

A map of a local hiking trail or somewhere you and your child like to explore

1. Before heading outside, talk about the route or trail you will take. Decide on the best path together.

2. While out and about, let your child be the keeper of the map.

3. Ask your child to make decisions about where you're going and what you'll do along the way.

HOW MANY CAN YOU HEAR?

Exploring nature involves hearing as well as seeing. And using nature to learn to count is the perfect way for your child to experience the world while learning number skills.

 EASY

What You'll Need

Just yourselves

1. Find a comfortable spot to sit outside with your child.

2. Listen to what's around you.

3. Ask your child to count the number of bird-calls they hear.

4. Can your child hear different types of bird-song? How many kinds can they hear?

RUN, WALK, OR CRAWL

Exploring new terrain may require depth perception, which is an important skill to develop. Find a hill, and then figure out together the best way to climb it. Should your child run up it? Walk? Crawl? Working this out helps develop depth perception, critical-thinking skills, and situational awareness.

EASY

What You'll Need

A hill

1. Find a hill. Decide together if it's big or small, steep or gentle, slippery, and so on.

2. Are there obstacles on the hill? Ask your child how they will navigate them.

3. Stand at the bottom of the hill. Work together to determine the safest and most fun way to climb the hill. Then do it!

BONUS ACTIVITY!

How many times can your child climb a hill? Have them count as they climb up and down.

MUD, DIRT, AND YOU!

"Why?" is one of the most commonly asked questions. Indulge your child's curiosity and desire to explore. What makes mud muddy and dirt dirty? Can your child find out with just a splash of water?

 EASY

What You'll Need

A clear plastic container

Water

1. Fill the container about halfway up with dry dirt.

2. Help your child make observations about the dirt. Ask:

   * *What color is the dirt? Is it more than one color?*
   * *Does it make a sound in the container? What kind of sound does it make?*
   * *How much dirt is in there? What happens if you pack down the dirt? Does it look like less dirt than if it's loose in the container?*

3. Add water to the container.

4. Ask your child to make observations by answering these questions:

   * *Has the color of the dirt changed?*
   * *Has the sound of the dirt in the container changed?*
   * *Has the amount of dirt in the container changed?*
   * *Do you think this is mud?*

5. Talk about the differences between dirt and mud. Experiment with different amounts of water to figure out how much water it takes before dirt becomes mud.

6. Keep the mud in the container over time. Ask your child how it looks in a day and in a week. Do they see any differences?

BONUS ACTIVITY!

Take a walk outside together and ask your child to point out as many different colors in nature as they can. Do they see their favorite color?

EYES CLOSED, FULL HANDS

Along with seeing and hearing, touch helps your child explore the world around them. It also helps them learn about trust.

 EASY

What You'll Need

Objects collected from nature

A blindfold (optional)

1. Ask your child to hold out their hand while blindfolded or with their eyes closed.

2. One by one, place objects in their outstretched hand.

3. Ask your child to guess what object they're holding.

4. Ask them how they knew. Encourage them to describe the shape, texture, smell, and sound.

5. Switch roles and try to guess what your child is placing in your hand. This will show your child that you trust them.

A BUG'S GUIDE TO LIFE

Bugs pollinate flowers and plants to give us food, nurture the ground to help the trees, and keep one another in check. Take this chance to help out even the smallest of creatures by creating a home for bugs.

 EASY

What You'll Need

Grass

Twigs

1. Scout out an area with your child where you might find bugs.

2. Look around together. Do you see spiders on the bark of a tree or worms rolling through the dirt?

3. Talk about what specific bugs need. Does a worm need wet ground? Does a spider need protection from the birds?

4. Using grass and twigs, help your child create a home to protect bugs from birds or other hungry critters.

DRESSING FOR SUCCESS

Explorers need the right clothing and gear when they head out into the world. The same is true of you and your child as you explore nature together. As you think about the weather outside, talk about the most appropriate clothes to wear on your adventures. Not only will you help foster your child's independent spirit, but you'll also be ready for any weather nature throws your way.

EASY

What You'll Need

An up-to-date weather forecast

Your child's wardrobe

1. Look at or listen to the day's weather forecast together.

2. Talk about what types of clothes you would typically wear in different weather conditions.

3. Go through your child's clothes and pull out three options for them to wear.

4. Let your child choose the clothing and dress themselves.

5. Head outside to test if the clothing choices are appropriate!

WHERE DID THAT COME FROM?

Put your deduction skills to the test as you and your child explore. During the fall, leaves and other objects drop from trees all the time. Some drop straight down while the wind moves others far from the tree. Together, can you find the tree that the leaves and other objects fell from?

 MEDIUM

What You'll Need

Outdoor space

1. Take a walk with your child, looking for leaves and other objects on the ground.

2. Let your child pick up the object and identify it. Is it a leaf? An acorn? A pine needle?

3. Work together to determine where the object might have come from.

   * *Is there a tree nearby?*
   * *Which way is the wind blowing—and did it blow the object far from the tree?*
   * *Is the acorn from the tree right above it or a different one?*
   * *How about the leaf?*

WILD-GOOSE CHASE

During the winter, snow helps us see animal tracks more easily than during the rest of the year. Create a trail of exploration in the snow for your child, using your footprints as a guide to an exciting adventure and a prize!

 MEDIUM

What You'll Need

A snowy space

A prize

1. Create a path in the snow, making sure that your footprints are visible. Add obstacles where possible.

2. Leave a prize at the end of the trail you have created. Keep it out of sight so that your child must follow the footsteps to find it.

3. Let your child follow the trail that has been left for them. If you want to walk the trail together, make sure your child leads the way.

OPEN OR CLOSED?

Exploration can be on a small scale as well as on a large scale. Think about all the plants growing in the spring. Take a closer look at them with a magnifying glass. What do you and your child see?

 EASY

What You'll Need

A magnifying glass

1. Teach your child how to use a magnifying glass. (Be sure to keep it out of direct sunlight so it doesn't create a fire hazard.)

2. Find flowers blooming and have your child look at them through a magnifying glass.

3. Ask questions that help your child explore these wonders of nature:

   * *What do you see in the magnifying glass that you can't see as easily with your eyes?*
   * *Do you see the same things in every flower?*
   * *Is the flower open or closed? Why?*
   * *Is the flower just starting to grow or is it completely in bloom? How can you tell?*

BONUS ACTIVITY!

Ask your child if they can find an object in nature that starts with the same letter as their first name.

COLORFUL NUMBERS

Nature is full of colors: the world is brimming with greens, browns, reds, yellows, blues, and so much more. Explore your backyard or a local park with your child and help them collect a number of items by color. For a challenge, have them collect objects that contain more than one color.

EASY

What You'll Need

Sticks, leaves, flowers, grass, or other objects in nature

An empty spot on the ground

1. Help your child choose a spot that is flat and wide to place all the collected objects.

2. Decide how many objects of each color your child should collect. For example: find one blue, two yellow, three red, four green, five brown, and six of more than one color.

3. Explore the nearby area and collect objects together. Bring them to your chosen spot.

4. Help your child create piles of the objects, sorted by color. Were they able to find the number of the colors you described?

HOW CAN I HELP?

The more you and your child explore nature, the more you may come across trash that doesn't belong there. Use this activity to teach how even one person can help make nature a better place to explore.

 EASY

What You'll Need

A small trash bag

1. Bring a small trash bag outdoors and take a walk with your child. Have a conversation about litter cleanup and what not to touch: glass, sharp objects, poop, unidentifiable objects, and so on.

2. Ask your child to help you put any trash you see into the bag.

3. Count how many pieces of trash you both have collected.

4. Talk about what you're doing:

   * *What can happen if the trash is left on the ground?*
   * *What are you helping in nature? Plants? Animals?*
   * *How does removing trash help nature?*
   * *How does it help us explore our world?*

5. Throw out the bag.

4

Nature Arts and Crafts

Children benefit from arts and crafts in several ways: it helps them develop fine motor skills, expand their vocabulary, express themselves, think critically, and be creative. And working with materials found in nature adds a new dimension to their creativity! By working with your child on these fun and easy outdoor art activities, you will also be creating wonderful memories.

TRACKS AND TRAILS

Ask your child to think about the animals they love and the tracks they make. Using their imagination, can they come up with a whole new animal with a new kind of track they leave behind?

 MEDIUM

What You'll Need

Paper

Crayons, colored pencils, pens, or markers

1. Together, talk about different animals and how they walk.

2. Help your child come up with a whole new animal. Is it a combination of animals, or something new altogether?

3. Ask your child to draw their animal and their animal's footprint.

4. Now create the new footprint in the dirt. How would your child feel if they came across that footprint in the wild?

5. Have your child draw where their new animal would live. In a nest in a tree? Underground in a hole? In a structure like a beaver's lodge or a human's home?

BONUS ACTIVITY!

Ask your child if they were a flower, what colors would they be? What shape? Have them draw themselves as a flower.

3D MAPMAKING

Making a map is fun! Encourage your child to create a 3D map using objects from a chosen location without using a pen or a pencil. This activity not only encourages a continued interest in the outdoors but also acts as a lesson in memory.

 CHALLENGING

What You'll Need

Cardboard

Glue

Objects from nature

1. Work together to find a location to map out.

2. With your child, collect objects from that location that can be used in a map.

3. Determine which objects can symbolize what landmarks on the map.

4. Help your child glue objects onto the piece of cardboard to represent the landmarks.

5. Can your child use the map to find their way around your chosen location?

ACORN PUPPETS

You and your child may find hundreds of acorns littering the ground beneath an oak tree. But if squirrels, chipmunks, or other creatures have been there, you may find just the tops of the acorns. These are perfect hats for finger puppets.

 MEDIUM

What You'll Need

Markers

20 acorn tops

1. Together, collect the tops of 20 acorns— one per finger for each of you.

2. Place a cap on the tip of each of your child's fingers.

3. Draw a face on their fingers, giving each finger a personality that matches its new cap.

4. Have your child perform a simple play based on their finger puppets.

5. Now switch! Let your child draw faces on your fingers to match your caps, then perform a play for them.

NATURE'S PAINTBRUSH

Conifers are trees that typically have needlelike leaves. Here's a fun way to turn conifer needles into paintbrushes.

 EASY

What You'll Need

Conifer needles

A twig

Glue

Twine

1. Collect healthy green conifer needles with your child.

2. If necessary, take the needles off sticks and twigs.

3. Help your child sort the needles by size and gather a bunch of similar-sized needles.

4. Together, glue the needles around one end of a twig, repeating until the needles cover the bottom of the twig.

5. Let the glue dry.

6. Once the glue has dried, help your child tie twine around the needles to form a paint-brush shape.

7. Glue the twine in place.

8. Ask your child to paint you a picture with their new paintbrush!

BERRY PAINTING

Nature is full of colors; some are brilliant and some are muted. Put some of those colors on paper with your child. Try making this paint together and have your child create a painting about nature from nature. (This paint can act like a dye, so be careful of clothes and hands.)

 MEDIUM

What You'll Need

Smock

1 cup strawberries, pokeberries, blueberries, blackberries, or huckleberries

2 cups

Fork

Strainer

Spoon

1 teaspoon white vinegar

Paper

Paintbrush

Water

1. Have your child (wearing a smock) put berries into a cup and squish them with a fork until a juice-like liquid is produced.

2. Help your child strain the juice into a clean cup. Let them separate the skin and any stems from the juice.

3. Add a teaspoon of white vinegar to the juice and mix with a spoon.

4. Let your child use the paint they made to create a scene from nature. Or paint a beautiful picture together!

LEAF PRESSING

Colorful leaves can be in our lives long past fall. Try this activity with your child so that you both can enjoy beautiful leaves all year long.

 EASY

What You'll Need

Paper

Leaves

Paint

Paintbrushes

1. Ask your child to paint one side of a leaf any way they want: with one color, many colors, with spots or lines, and so on.

2. Before the paint dries, help them place the painted side of the leaf on a piece of paper and press down.

3. Tell them to carefully lift the leaf off the paper.

4. Repeat as many times as your child likes.

5. Let the artwork dry fully before hanging it up for all to see!

BONUS ACTIVITY!

Have your child draw a tree that has more than one shape. Does it look like a real tree, or something out of their imagination?

MARK YOUR WAY

Trail markers help us find our way on trails. Some are carved into trees and wood while others are written on metal or plastic signs. Have you and your child ever seen any while hiking? Here's how to create trail markers that you both can use to guide others on your favorite path. (Be sure to get permission from the trail owner and take down your markers when you're done.)

 MEDIUM

What You'll Need

Paper or cardboard

Crayons, colored pencils, pens, or markers

Tape

Scissors

Skewers

1. Talk about a destination with your child. Where will your trail lead, and what route will it take?

2. Help your child decide what shape their trail marker will be, then draw the outline on a piece of paper.

3. Put several pieces of paper behind the one with the outline and cut out several trail markers at once, or cut several pieces of cardboard into the desired shape.

4. Let your child fill in the trail markers using arrows, colors, objects, and words (with your help) for directions.

5. Help them tape the trail markers to skewers.

6. Together, plant your trail markers outside to help others follow your path.

CONE YOU HEAR THE BIRDS?

While listening to birds and seeing them soar through the sky can be fun for your child, seeing them close-up can be thrilling. Leave a gift for the birds using only a few items, and watch your child observe them with wonder.

 MEDIUM

What You'll Need

Twine

Pine cone

Plastic knife

Peanut butter
(or peanut-free
sticky alternative)

Birdseed

1. Attach a loop of twine to the top of the pine cone so you can hang it from a bush or a tree.

2. Using a plastic knife, help your child cover the pine cone with peanut butter.

3. Let your child sprinkle birdseed over the peanut butter or roll the pine cone in birdseed until it is completely covered.

4. Talk about where to hang the bird feeder. Do you want to be able to see it from indoors?

5. Hang up the bird feeder and watch all your new friends together.

6. Observe the kinds of birds that stop by the bird feeder. Have your child count the number of different birds they see at one time.

JUMPING OFF THE CANVAS

Head outside to paint—in the snow! Have your child turn the snowy ground into their paper and use squeeze bottles as brushes.

 EASY

What You'll Need

Squeeze bottles (like old ketchup or mustard bottles)

Liquid food coloring

Water

Snow on the ground

1. Put a few drops of food coloring into each of the squeeze bottles. Each bottle gets its own color.

2. Ask your child to fill the squeeze bottles with water.

3. Head outside together with the squeeze bottles and watch your child paint a masterpiece in the snow!

BONUS ACTIVITY!

Create shapes (triangles, circles, squares) in the snow with your footprints. See if your child can identify them.

BUTTERFLY WINGS

Butterflies have symmetrical wings, which make their colors and beauty twice as nice. Have your child create a butterfly of their own, keeping the symmetry that makes a butterfly a butterfly.

 MEDIUM

What You'll Need

A twig or small stick

Leaves

Glue

Paint

1. Help your child find a twig for the body of the butterfly and leaves for the wings.

2. Have them paint a face on one side of the twig.

3. Show them how to create wings using the leaves. Glue the leaves onto the twig.

4. Let your child paint the leaves to create the butterfly's wings, keeping a butterfly's symmetry in mind.

FEATHERBRAINED FASHION

Young children imagine fancy clothes when they play dress-up. Show them how they can design fabulous clothing not from fabric but with objects they find in nature. Allowing children to use objects in new ways helps them think creatively and develop their problem-solving skills.

 EASY

What You'll Need

Paper

Crayons, colored pencils, pens, or markers

Feathers, leaves, and other found materials

Glue

1. Help your child draw a simple picture of themselves on a piece of paper.

2. Discuss what they are getting dressed for. Are they an award winner about to give a speech? Are they an artist about to show their artwork to the world? Are they a member of the royal family on their way to a ball? Or are they something else altogether?

3. Using the found objects, let your child create an outfit for their picture.

4. Help them glue the objects into place.

5. After the glue has dried, have your child write their name on the top of the page. Write the reason for their fancy outfit for them.

TWIG FRAME

Family photos are treasured mementos, and a family photo surrounded by a child's homemade frame is the most treasured of all. Do you have a photo that you want to display? Draw attention to it by having your child create a frame for it out of twigs.

EASY

What You'll Need

Twigs

Glue

Paint and glitter (optional)

A photo

1. Search for twigs of like sizes with your child and group them together.

2. Have your child create a rectangle or square the size of the photo out of the groups of twigs.

3. Glue the bundles of twigs together.

4. Once the glue has dried, have your child glue the corners of the bundles together to complete the rectangle or square.

5. Glue the photo, facing forward, to the back of the frame once the rectangle or square has dried.

6. Let your child decorate the frame with paint and glitter to give it real personality!

NATURE DOLLS

As long as there has been corn, there have been dolls made out of the husks. Since not everyone has access to corn husks these days, this activity uses other materials from nature to make a doll.

 CHALLENGING

What You'll Need

A rock or pine cone

Twigs, leaves, or other found materials

Glue

Paint

Paintbrush

1. Let your child choose a rock or a pine cone for the head of their doll.

2. Have them glue a sturdy stick to the rock or pine cone for the body and other sticks for the arms and legs.

3. Ask them to create clothes out of leaves or other found materials and glue them onto their doll.

4. Have them decorate their doll with paint and ask them to give it a name.

FAMILY FLAG

Your child has probably seen their country's flag, and maybe even their state's flag. But do they have a family flag? Here's their chance to create a family flag from nature and in nature.

 EASY

What You'll Need

A patch of grass or dirt

Sticks

Stones

Leaves

Berries, flowers, and other colorful objects

1. Help your child find a small patch of grass or dirt to lay out their family flag.

2. Together, brainstorm what your family flag should look like.

3. If needed, offer help as your child creates a unique family flag on the ground from objects collected from nature.

4. Ask your child to explain why they designed the flag the way they did.

5

Playful Nature Games

The outdoors are huge and wild and inspire children to get their wiggles out. Kids can run over the uneven grass to develop motor skills, kick their shoes to develop coordination, and pick up sticks to build muscles. The activities in this chapter provide an outlet for kids who want to run and jump and incorporate nature into their play.

THE PUDDLE JUMP

Channel the Olympic triple jump spirit into the puddle jump. Score your child on the biggest splash, highest jump, and of course, muddiest. Some kids might resist getting wet and muddy; show them how fun a rainy day can really be.

EASY

What You'll Need

Puddles

Rainy-day clothes, coats, and boots

1. Find a big puddle together.

2. Create categories of competition: biggest one-foot splash, biggest two-foot splash, biggest splash with a rock, best jump over the puddle, muddiest boots, and so on.

3. Give your child points for each category on a scale from 1 to 10 like an Olympic judge; join in the fun to make it a real competition!

BONUS ACTIVITY!

Have your child run from tree to tree, counting each one as they touch it to practice early math skills.

IF IT WALKS LIKE A DUCK

Walking over uneven ground can be difficult for children. This activity helps kids develop that skill while having fun learning more about the animals around us.

 MEDIUM

What You'll Need

Open space

Rope or cones to make a starting and finishing line

1. Create a starting and finishing line in an open space.

2. Have your child stand ready at the starting line. Call out the name of an animal.

3. Have your child race from start to finish, walking or running like that animal.

4. Repeat this as many times as you would like, calling out the names of different animals.

NATURE CHARADES

Ideal for both outdoor and indoor play, this activity helps to encourage a sense of excitement around nature (even when you and your child can't get outside). This silent game helps children develop their nonverbal communication skills and eventually their all-around communication skills.

 MEDIUM

What You'll Need

Names of common, easily identifiable land animals (lion, monkey, elephant), plants (flower, bush, tree), and birds (flamingo, chicken, duck) on small pieces of paper (one per piece of paper)

A bowl to hold the pieces of paper

1. Let your child choose a piece of paper from the bowl. Whisper what's written on the paper in their ear so no one else can hear.

2. Tell your child to pantomime that animal, plant, or bird. To indicate an animal, silently roar. To indicate a plant, pretend to grow up from the ground. To indicate a bird, flap your arms like wings. Then tell them to act out something specific about their animal, plant, or bird.

3. Have others try to guess what your child is impersonating.

4. Whoever gets it right is the next presenter.

FREE PLAY

Child-directed play is an important part of cultivating a child's sense of freedom with the outdoors. That does not mean boundaries don't exist. Creating a boundary allows freedom without worry. Create boundaries, practice stopping at them together, and then hand the reins of play over to your child.

 EASY

What You'll Need

Cones

1. Place the cones in a circle or square formation with your child.

2. Walk the cone boundary together, talking about all the fun things your child can do inside of it.

3. Practice running up to the cones and stopping with one another.

4. Tell your child that they get to decide what you are going to play.

5. Follow their lead (and don't say no inside the cone boundary).

TREE TO TREE

Choosing words to describe an action can be hard sometimes. Work together to create a racecourse that travels from tree to tree using only words. Using descriptive words helps develop your child's communication skills—both listening and speaking—while running around and having fun.

 MEDIUM

What You'll Need

A wooded area

Rope

1. Create a starting point by placing a rope on the ground.

2. Stand at the starting point with your child and describe the first place your child will go, using nothing but words.

3. Have your child run to the first location. Now describe the next stop on the course, again using only words.

4. Have your child race to the second location. Describe the rest of the course in steps, and have your child follow your instructions until they are tired.

5. Switch places. Can your child describe where you should go?

BONUS ACTIVITY!

Make a racecourse in a shape like a circle or square. Can your child figure out what shape it is?

RIBBIT, RIBBIT

Everyone loves to jump around. It can be even more fun to hop around!
See how far your child can go, hopping a mile in frogs' legs.

 EASY

What You'll Need

Outdoor space

Pieces of bark

1. Have your child do their best impression of a frog's croak and a frog's hop.

2. Place the bark on the ground about a foot apart.

3. Have your child hop from bark to bark, counting the pieces of bark they land on in a frog's croak.

SHOE GOLF

You and your child don't need clubs or a tee time for golf when your shoes are readily available! Using tree trunks as holes and shoes as balls, you can both play shoe golf as a new way to explore the outdoors. And kicking while standing on one foot helps your child practice balance and foot-eye coordination.

 MEDIUM

What You'll Need

A wooded space

Shoes that can get dirty and damaged

A rope

1. Place the rope on the ground to create a starting point.

2. Ask your child to choose a tree or other landmark as the first hole.

3. Come up with a par, or the number of times a shoe can be kicked to hit the tree.

4. Take turns with your child kicking your shoes at the tree. Try to hit the tree with your shoe within par. (Make sure no one is between the kicker and the tree.)

5. If you and your child don't hit the tree on the first kick, hop over to your shoes and keep trying.

6. Go through five trees or landmarks, moving the rope to create a new starting point for each one.

TREE DANCES

Sometimes kids just have to get their sillies out. Let your child get swept away by the breeze and dance like a tree in the wind.

 EASY

What You'll Need

Open space

1. Have your child place their feet firmly on the ground. Call this "rooting their feet."

2. Talk about how the wind blows from different directions.

3. Together, wave your arms like a tree in the wind.

4. What happens if the wind blows from a different direction? What if the wind is a gentle breeze? A tornado? Have your child act out how a tree would behave in those situations.

BURROW TO BUSH

Best played with the whole family, this activity lets your child step into the paws of an animal and run wild.

 CHALLENGING

What You'll Need

A square-shaped field or open space

Multiple players

1. Name one player the wolf pack leader. The rest of the players are the pack.

2. Designate one side of the field the burrow and the opposite side the bush.

3. The two remaining sides (opposite each other) are the lake and the hill.

4. When the pack leader calls out one of the locations, the pack runs toward it and stops when they reach it.

5. For an added challenge, make running to the location a race.

6. When the pack leader yells out the words "Wolf Pack!" all players must stop where they are and look serious.

7. The pack leader then tries to get them to laugh.

8. Whoever laughs first becomes the pack leader.

FOOTPRINTS IN THE FOREST

Using animal footprints, create an obstacle course outdoors for your child. Help them put their crab-walking, bear-hugging, and wolf-howling skills to the test by following the animals' footsteps.

 MEDIUM

What You'll Need

Open space

Hand-drawn tracks of bears, crabs, wolves, ducks, and deer

A rope

1. Work together to draw different types of animal tracks. Each one gets its own piece of paper.

2. Create an obstacle course outside by placing the animal tracks on the ground about six feet apart.

3. Put the rope on the ground as a starting point.

4. Have your child run from the starting point all the way through the course. When they get to an animal track they must complete a task. (You can make up your own tasks that are tailored to your child, or use the ones below.)

   * *Give a bear hug when you reach the bear tracks.*
   * *Circle the crab tracks five times while crab walking.*
   * *Howl at the wolf tracks.*
   * *Say five words that begin with the letter D at the duck tracks.*
   * *Jump over the deer tracks 10 times.*

PINE CONE BASEBALL

Here's a twist on an American pastime! Help your child enjoy the game of baseball—but with objects from nature and in nature.

 MEDIUM

What You'll Need

A large, heavy stick

Round pine cones

Trees for bases

1. Determine which trees are the bases.

2. Have your child stand at "home plate" with the stick as a bat. (Talk about stick safety first.)

3. Gently pitch the pine cone ball to your child.

4. If your child hits the pine cone, encourage them to run the bases. If not, pitch again until your child scores a run.

BONUS ACTIVITY!

Collect as many pine cones as you and your child can hold and organize them by size. Together, guess which ones your child can throw the farthest, and then see if you're right!

TIC-TAC-TREE

Take hand-eye coordination to the next level with a fun way to play a traditional game with nature.

 MEDIUM

What You'll Need

Four large sticks, all the same size

Pine cones

Stones or other small throwable objects

1. Have your child help you place the four sticks in an overlapping pattern to create a three-by-three grid.

2. Ask your child to make a pile of pine cones for them and a pile of stones for you.

3. On the count of three, you both throw your object at the grid, trying to land in one of the boxes.

4. Once the object has landed, throw the next one.

5. The first player to create a single line with their objects is the winner.

LEAF KITE

During autumn, the crisp fall breeze helps leaves fall to the ground. Show your child how to use that wind to lift their leaf kite high into the sky.

 MEDIUM

What You'll Need

Fall leaves

Six inches of thread or twine

A thick plastic needle

1. Help your child thread their needle with the twine.

2. Have them pierce the leaf with the needle so that the twine ends up almost entirely through the leaf; make sure about two inches of twine remains on the other side of the leaf.

3. Show them how to take the needle off the twine and tie a knot on both sides of the leaf.

4. Let them run around with their new kite, seeing how high the wind will take it.

6

Use Your Imagination

Mountains are tall and oceans are deep, but with a child's imagination, they grow taller and deeper. The mountains become sleeping dragons and the child becomes a hero. Children learn to process the world around them through imaginative play. As an important part of their social-emotional development, imaginative play also helps them learn how to treat other people and determine how they like to be treated. This chapter provides activities for children to exercise their imagination.

NEW IN TOWN

There are so many animals in the world, and the future could allow for even more. Help your child come up with a whole new animal—no limit to their imagination!

EASY

What You'll Need

Space to run

Paper

Crayons, colored pencils, pens, or markers

1. Help your child think up a new animal.

2. Is it a mix of other animals, or something new altogether?

3. Ask your child to show you how that animal would walk and run and what it would sound like.

4. Ask them detailed questions about their animal:

   * *What would it eat?*
   * *Where would it sleep?*
   * *What animals would it be afraid of?*

5. Help your child come up with a name for their new animal.

6. Have your child draw a picture of their animal and where it lives.

BONUS ACTIVITY!

Have your child name a real animal using the first letter in their first name.

INTERVIEW WITH AN ANIMAL

Journalists interview everyone who has a story. If your child had a chance to interview their favorite animal, what would that animal say? What questions would your child ask? Take turns playing animal and interviewer with them.

 EASY

What You'll Need

Space to sit outside opposite each other

1. Arrange an outdoor space to mimic a television interview. Make sure you and your child are facing each other.

2. Have your child choose an animal to be for the interview.

3. Acting as the journalist, ask your child questions about their animal. Ask them to demonstrate their walk (or flight), their sounds, and the way they eat.

4. When your child has answered all your questions, switch roles: your child becomes the journalist and you become the animal.

NATURE CAKE

Young children love to dig in the dirt and create imaginary goodies to eat. Provide your child with a few tools from the kitchen and watch what they bake!

EASY

What You'll Need

Dirt or mud

A medium-sized baking pan

A spoon

Flowers, acorns, leaves, and other decorative objects from nature

Plastic or paper plates and plastic forks

1. Have your child fill a baking pan with mud or dirt, spoonful by spoonful, until they've made a cake. Make sure they tamp down the mud or dirt so the top is level.

2. Ask them to decorate their cake with objects found in nature. Do they like colorful flowers? Sticks to represent candles on a birthday cake?

3. Help your child scoop out pieces of cake on plates for each of you to pretend to eat.

RUNNING WITH THE WOLVES

Empathetic people know how to walk a mile in someone else's shoes. Here's a fun way for your child to play a game in another animal's paws, or wings, or even fins.

EASY

What You'll Need

Open space

Cones

1. Mark boundaries for the area of play with the cones.

2. Let your child decide who is the predator and who is the prey.

3. Help your child choose an appropriate animal as a predator and an appropriate animal as prey. Each player spends the game moving as that animal.

4. The predator tries to tag the prey. Once tagged, the prey becomes the predator and both players choose a new animal.

BONUS ACTIVITY!

Together, count how many animals you see in one day. Count again the next day. Help your child figure out the reasons for the difference in numbers between the days.

FREAKY FRIDAY

Has your child ever wondered what it would be like to see the world through an animal's eyes? How about walking a mile in another creature's paws? What if an animal got to walk in your child's shoes? Let your child play as if they switched places with an animal.

 EASY

What You'll Need

Open space

1. Let your child choose an animal to switch places with.

2. Help them think about that animal's environment: where they live, what they eat, and so on.

3. Help your child think about their own environment: where they live, what they eat, etc. Does your child share any similarities with that animal?

4. Have your child act out how they would live their life as that animal.

WORLD TRAVELER

The world is full of ecosystems—groups of living things that live and interact with each other in a particular environment. An ecosystem can be as small as a backyard or as vast as a desert. What would happen if an animal from a very different ecosystem were to visit yours?

 MEDIUM

What You'll Need

Open space

1. Ask your child to describe their ecosystem and the animals that live in it.

2. Help them describe an ecosystem that is very different from theirs.

3. Have your child act out how an animal from that vastly different ecosystem would react to where they live.

UPSIDE DOWN AND INSIDE OUT

Sometimes the world can seem upside down. Push your child's imagination to the limit: What would the world look like if fish flew and birds swam?

EASY

What You'll Need

Open space

1. Ask your child to tell you a story about what the world would look like if they lived in the sky or spoke to talking animals, or something else upside down in nature.

2. Have them act out part of their story.

3. Ask your child to give you a kooky premise for your story. Tell your story and act it out.

BONUS ACTIVITY!

Have your child imagine specific animals in the wrong environments. What colors would flying fish or underwater birds be? What sounds would they make?

WHAT THE MOON SEES

Your child can explain what they see from their perspective, but what about from someone else's perspective? Or some*thing* else's? As you take a walk together, ask your child to look up and imagine what the moon sees.

EASY

What You'll Need

A place to walk

1. Ask your child to list the things they see and imagine what they must look like from above.

2. Ask them questions about the moon's perspective:

   * *Does the moon have favorite things to look at?*
   * *Does it see things differently in the day versus the night?*

3. Have your child tell you a story about what the moon sees.

CREATURE, CREATURE, CROSS MY JUNGLE

Some people learn best when they are moving. This opens up a whole new fun world of games. Let your child's imagination run wild while playing a game.

 CHALLENGING

What You'll Need

A field

Three to four players (or more)

1. Assign one player the zookeeper role. This player stands in the middle of the field. All the other players line up shoulder to shoulder on one side of the field.

2. Each player chooses to be an animal (but keeps it to themselves).

3. The zookeeper yells out an animal characteristic (like a trunk, wings, etc.).

4. Any "animals" who have that characteristic try to run across the field without getting tagged by the zookeeper. They are safe if they reach the opposite side of the field without being tagged.

5. If the zookeeper tags an animal, they must guess what type of animal they've caught.

6. If the zookeeper is correct, the animal is stuck in place and can catch others without moving their feet. If the zookeeper is wrong, the animal can keep running.

7. The last animal running can choose to be the next zookeeper or stay an animal.

8. Everyone chooses a new animal each round.

ANIMAL SCHOOL

Whether or not your child has started school, they probably know what school entails. But what would an animal school look like? Have them imagine it when you're outside with animals all around you.

EASY

What You'll Need

Paper

Crayons, colored pencils, pens, or markers

1. Help your child imagine a classroom full of animals. Have them look around for inspiration.

2. Have your child answer these questions about a classroom full of animals to stretch their imagination:

   * *Which animal would be the teacher?*
   * *Which animals would pay attention in class more than others?*
   * *What kinds of desks would the animals sit at in the classroom?*
   * *What would the classroom look like?*

IF THE FOREST COULD TALK

Trees see and hear everything. Instill a sense of ownership in the outdoors by having your child give a tree a name and a backstory.

 EASY

What You'll Need

A tree

1. Have your child choose a tree.

2. Ask your child to give their tree a name.

3. Ask your child how old the tree is.

4. Have your child tell a story about the tree.

   * *What is its favorite food?*
   * *What is its favorite school subject?*
   * *Does it like reading?*
   * *Who are its friends?*
   * *Does it have a hobby?*

5. Make sure you and your child say hello to the tree every time you pass it.

RULER OF THE FOREST

Your child wakes up tomorrow as ruler of the forest. What would they do as the leader of all the animals in nature?

 EASY

What You'll Need

A tree stump or large flat rock or other object to serve as a throne

1. Help your child find a place to sit that serves as a throne.

2. Talk about which animals live in their kingdom.

3. Ask your child what they will do to make the forest a better place for all the animals. How can they help keep nature clean and animals healthy?

MASTER CHEF

Cooking and serving delicious play food at an imaginary restaurant is a childhood staple. Bring the kitchen outside and see what your child creates!

EASY

What You'll Need

Found objects

Paper plates

Plastic forks and spoons

Mud

Grass

1. Together, find objects outside that will create interesting dishes at your child's restaurant.

2. Talk about the name of your child's restaurant. Will it be named after you, your child, or something else altogether?

3. Have your child use the mud, grass, and other found objects to make their favorite dishes or new dishes from their imagination and serve them on the paper plates.

4. Pretend to eat your meal together.

7

Build and Grow

Young children love to stack and build and grow (and knock down!) and can do all that with nature. Building and growing require patience, an important ability for kids to develop. Whether they're building shelter from the elements or growing flowers, children will learn to be patient and look forward to their accomplishments. And as you build and grow along with your child, you will forge a deep bond together. Here's how.

SNOWCANOS

The best structures to build are structures that you and your child can interact with. Help your child build a snow volcano and then watch it erupt!

 MEDIUM

What You'll Need

Snow

Cup

4 tablespoons baking soda

1 teaspoon dish soap

Food coloring

Stick

1 cup vinegar

1. Help your child build a volcano using snow outside. Be sure to create a dip (or well) in the middle. Place the cup inside the well.

2. Have them pour the baking soda, dish soap, a few drops of food coloring, and about a cup of snow into the cup in the well.

3. Mix the ingredients with a stick until combined.

4. Add the vinegar (best if the adult does this), step aside quickly, and let 'er blow!

BONUS ACTIVITY!

Animals of all kinds build their homes in, around, on, and under trees. Together, count the number of animals that call a tree home.

SHELTER FROM THE STORM

Although you and your child will most likely be able to rush indoors if the weather turns bad, it's always best to be prepared on a less-than-ideal day. Here's how to build shelter together to protect you (during a light rain—never a thunderstorm).

 MEDIUM

What You'll Need

A tarp

Two feet of rope

1. Together, locate a space between multiple sturdy trees.

2. Help your child tie the rope to the tarp using any knot, including the one used to tie your shoes.

3. Let your child wrap the rope around a tree at the tallest height possible.

4. Help your child tie the rope to the tree.

5. Repeat steps one through four for the other three sides of the tarp, making sure one half of the tarp is lower than the other half (to protect it from wind and to help rain run off the top).

6. Crawl into the shelter together to admire your child's work!

FAIRY HOMES

Almost every culture in the world has a myth that revolves around a fairy or fairylike creature. Bring those stories to life and ignite your child's imagination by having them build a home for the fairies who live near them.

 MEDIUM

What You'll Need

Sticks, twigs, or other objects in nature

1. Find a space protected from the elements such as the wind.

2. Together, pick up small sticks and twigs and other objects in nature (like leaves, acorns, and so on) that your child can use to create the fairy home.

3. Help your child create a miniature home with sticks and twigs. For walls, place the sticks in a pile, lean the sticks against one another, or lean them against the base of a tree.

4. Ask your child if they can make the home more welcoming. Can they add little stones to create a walkway or moss to create a bed?

BOAT BUILDING

Ahoy, maties! There is so much to see on the high seas. Have your child combine a bit of engineering with a spark of imagination to create a grand adventure.

 CHALLENGING

What You'll Need

A small action figure or other small toys

Aluminum foil

Glue

Leaves

Sticks and twigs

Markers for decoration

A puddle or other small body of water

1. Let your child choose a small action figure or other toy as their ship's captain. (They will use this figure to help them build their ship to its scale.)

2. Ask your child to shape aluminum foil until they like the shape for their boat.

3. Have your child glue leaves to the aluminum foil boat to build the exterior of the ship.

4. Once the glue has dried, have your child glue sticks and twigs to cover the leaves.

5. Ask your child to name their ship and decorate it with whatever they want.

6. Tell them to place their captain in their boat and set sail in the great outdoors!

OUTSIDE TERRARIUM

Help your child create a world all their own by making a terrarium. Just like an aquarium full of fish shows them a fraction of the ocean, a terrarium shows them a part of the world. Bring the materials outside and have your child use nature as inspiration.

 MEDIUM

What You'll Need

Pebbles

A glass container

Charcoal

Dirt

Small plants (succulents work well)

Moss

Small toys (optional)

1. Have your child put pebbles in the bottom of the glass container.

2. Have them add a layer of charcoal on top of the pebbles. (The charcoal helps filter the soil and the air in the terrarium, allowing the ecosystem to thrive.)

3. Above the charcoal, have them add a much thicker layer of soil that fills about half the container.

4. Together, place their plants into the soil.

5. Have your child add the moss and any small toys they desire.

6. Show your child how to lightly water their terrarium.

7. Place the terrarium out of direct sunlight and enjoy your child's very own world together!

BUILDING A QUINZEE

Winter can be an intimidating time to go outside. Don't let the snow or cold deter you! Build a shelter made out of snow with your child and enjoy the space together.

 CHALLENGING

What You'll Need

Shovels

Snow

Several two-foot-long sticks

A large stick (about the size of an adult leg)

1. Together, use shovels to make a large pile of snow. The pile should be big enough so that when it is hollowed out you can both fit inside. Make sure the pile is dome-shaped at the top. (A flat ceiling will collapse.)

2. Place a large stick in the center of the pile so that you will be able to find your quinzee later.

3. Have your child push the two-foot-long sticks from the outside of the snow pile to the inside, a few feet away from each other. (This way you'll have walls with an even thickness when you shovel out the pile.)

4. Compact the snow by pushing it with the flat side of a shovel and let it sit for an hour. This helps with structural integrity.

5. Dig an entrance hole with your child and use it to shovel your way into the pile.

6. Together, hollow out the pile, using the two-foot-long sticks to gauge how high up to shovel. When you encounter a stick, stop shoveling.

7. Once you and your child have hollowed out your snow pile, you have your quinzee!

SNOWBODY ELSE

Has your child heard of selfies? Maybe they've seen a family portrait somewhere. Give your family new life by creating snowfies, selfies made out of snow! Re-create your family in snowman form together.

 CHALLENGING

What You'll Need

Snow

Props (for eyes, nose, buttons, and so on)

1. Help your child roll a large ball of snow for the base of each snowperson.

2. Work together to make a smaller ball of snow for each snowperson's torso and place it on top of the larger ones.

3. Let your child make a small ball for each head. Help them place it on the top of each torso.

4. Watch your child use the props to re-create each snowperson in your family.

5. Take a picture of them with their creations!

FOOT TOWER

Building a tower with blocks or rocks requires motor skills, but building a tower with your feet requires imagination along with dexterity. Build a tower of feet with your child to stretch their imagination and touch the sky!

EASY

What You'll Need

Your feet and your child's feet

1. Lie on the ground with your feet touching each other's.

2. Place one foot square on the ground. Have your child place their foot on top of yours, their heel touching your toes. Next, gently place your other foot on top of their foot. Continue this pattern, moving the bottom foot to the top when it's your turn.

3. Keep building the tower without lowering your feet to the ground. How high can you go?

BONUS ACTIVITY!

Have you and your child seen a few rocks stacked up on top of one another when you've gone hiking? These are called cairns. Show your child how to build their own cairn by stacking rocks one on top of the other into a small tower.

STICKS AND STONES SUNDIAL

Building a sundial lets your child use nature to learn about and tell time. Help them create a simple sundial to keep track of the hours in their busy day.

MEDIUM

What You'll Need

A level, sunny outdoor space

One large stick

12 medium-sized rocks

Marker (optional)

1. Help your child find a sunny, flat space for the sundial.

2. Have them push the stick into the ground, straight up and down, so that it doesn't wobble.

3. Starting around 7:00 a.m., have your child place a rock at the tip of the shadow cast by the stick.

4. Return every hour in daylight to place a new rock at the top of the shadow. Mark the time on the stone (say, 3:00 p.m.) with the marker, if noting it will help your child.

5. When your child wants to tell the time, show them how the shadow gives them the time of day!

GARDEN TOWER

Here's a twist on container gardening to make it more fun for you and your child. Build a tower of containers and plants for a dramatic new garden.

 MEDIUM

What You'll Need

Four flowerpots
of varying sizes

Potting soil

A spade or large spoon

Plants

1. Have your child place the largest flowerpot on the ground and fill it with potting soil with the spade or spoon.

2. Help them flatten the soil in the middle of the pot and put the next-largest flowerpot on top.

3. Repeat steps one and two with the two remaining flowerpots, saving the smallest pot for the top.

4. Help your child place plants in the top pot and in the exposed dirt at the edges of all the flowerpots and watch their tower grow!

MUD BRICK HOUSE

Building with bricks is great for older kids, but what can younger kids build with? Try mud bricks! Make mud bricks with your child and then let their imagination run wild with all the structures they can build.

 EASY

What You'll Need

A big spoon

Several ice cube trays

Mud

1. Have your child use a big spoon to fill a few ice cube trays with mud. Help them pack down the mud into the trays.

2. Let the trays sit in the sun for a few hours to dry the mud.

3. Empty the mud bricks from the trays onto the ground.

4. Encourage your child to create different kinds of structures from the bricks. Can they build a tower? A house?

BONUS ACTIVITY!

Using stones, have your child form the first letter of their name on the ground.

LEAVE NO TRACE

Different outdoor areas have different rules about what you can leave behind and where. Before you head out, look over the rules of the outdoor space together. Some places adhere to a Leave No Trace policy: you must take out what you bring in. This can also apply to things you have built and leaving no trace on the outdoors you have touched. Work on personal responsibility together and have fun destroying whatever you just made.

EASY

What You'll Need

Building materials appropriate for your environment (sticks, leaves, sand, and so on)

1. Talk about the idea of Leave No Trace and what that means.

2. Find a place outdoors where you can build a small structure with your child.

3. Build a small structure together, whether it's a pile of leaves, a sculpture made of sticks, or a castle of sand.

4. Destroy what you have created, leaving the space just as you both found it.

8

Music to My Ears

Music is a part of the world. Stand anywhere outside and you will hear a symphony! The sound of the birds, wind, and trees coalesce to make the world sing. Spend time with your child outside, listening to the sounds of the world and adding a few of your own. Here are fun activities for imitating and creating music in nature together.

CAPTURE A MUSICAL MOMENT

Nature will probably always be an important part of your child's life, and nature's sounds can remind them of what they did outside that day or in years past. Have your child identify the music of nature, and capture it so you can return it to them in the future.

EASY

What You'll Need

A phone with an audio recording app or other audio recorder

1. Take your audio recording device with you when you head outdoors with your child.

2. Take a walk together and talk about the sounds you hear and would like to record. Does your child like the sound of running water? The call of birds? The croaking of frogs? The sound of your feet as you hike?

3. Let your child decide what to record, and save the sounds as best you can. Gift them back to your child on a rainy indoor day, when they need inspiration from nature, or when they are older as precious memories.

BONUS ACTIVITY!

Set a timer for 30 seconds. Sit quietly with your child and count the number of sounds you hear before your 30 seconds are up. Decide if you want to count just nature sounds or if other sounds—like cars and airplanes—will be part of your list.

THE PERCUSSION SECTION

Kids love to hit things with a stick, but do they listen to the sounds they make? Encourage their musical curiosity by having them hit different-sized rocks and logs. An additional benefit: holding on to the stick helps develop the same muscles in their hands that they will use to hold a pencil in school.

EASY

What You'll Need

Two similar-sized sticks

Rocks

Logs

1. Help your child find two sticks similar in length that they can use as drumsticks. (Remind them about stick safety!)

2. Let them hit various rocks and logs and listen to the sounds they make. How does the sound differ from a big log to a little log? How does a rock sound differ from a log sound?

3. Have your child collect the best-sounding rocks and logs to create their own natural drum kit!

CHIRP AND REPEAT

With the changing of the seasons comes a different set of birds. Listen together to the ones you can hear and have your child do their best impressions.

EASY

What You'll Need

A quiet spot outside

1. Find a quiet, comfortable spot together outside.

2. Listen to the birds.

3. After listening for a few minutes, ask your child to do their best impression of what they've heard: Can they sound like the chickadee repeating its own name? Can they caw like a crow? Honk like a Canada goose or quack like a duck?

4. If a bird responds to your child's call (or seems to respond), ask your child to imagine what the bird is saying to them.

NATURE'S MARACAS

Objects in nature can make beautiful sounds, and they can make lots of different sounds depending on the object and the container that holds it. Help your child make several maracas from nature and compare what you hear.

 MEDIUM

What You'll Need

Several small containers with lids made of different materials: metal, cardboard, and plastic

Acorns, sticks, and pebbles

1. Together, collect objects from nature that are likely to make sounds when shaken in a container.

2. Help your child decide which object they'll use first (such as acorns).

3. Have your child drop a handful of that object into containers of metal, plastic, and cardboard, and cover each with a lid.

4. Let your child shake each container, listening carefully to how each one sounds. Do they sound alike? Or do they sound different, depending on the container?

5. Have your child put another object (pebbles, for example) into the containers to determine if the object inside makes the sound different.

CATCH A TUNE

Help your child think of a song they love and bring it into nature (and nature into it!). Let them turn a favorite song into a nature memory with new words.

 MEDIUM

What You'll Need

Your child's favorite song

Paper

Pen or pencil

1. Have your child choose their favorite song. Sing it together to remember the music.

2. Help your child decide on a nature topic for their new song: Is it a hike they loved? A favorite outdoor space? An animal they like to watch? Revisit the place or animal or object to help them come up with new lyrics.

3. Work with your child to write down the new lyrics of the song to match their topic.

4. Together, sing their new song out loud for all to hear!

THE SOUND OF WATER

Why do children always want to throw rocks into the water? (Why do we?) Encourage your child's desire by comparing and contrasting the sounds different rocks make when they hit the water.

EASY

What You'll Need

Rocks

A body of water

1. Together, collect rocks in various shapes and sizes.

2. Have your child sort the rocks into groups based on size.

3. Talk about which rocks will make the biggest splash and the loudest sound. Will the sounds differ based on the size of the rock?

4. Ask your child to throw the rocks into the water in ascending order of size.

5. After each throw, take a moment to notice what the rock sounded like when it hit the water. Was the sound a plop? A thud? Or something else? Did the size of the rock determine the sound? Did the size of the splash correlate with the loudness of the sound?

NATURE STICK

Nature offers many opportunities to make music, whether it's a simple imitation of a bird call or a nature stick filled with found objects. Help your child build this music maker to create joyful noise!

 MEDIUM

What You'll Need

Paper

Scissors

A paper towel tube

Glue

Pebbles, sticks, bark, shells, acorns, seed pods, and other small found objects

Aluminum foil

Crayons, colored pencils, pens, or markers

1. Help your child cut two circles out of the paper to cover both ends of the paper towel tube. Make sure the circle is bigger than the diameter of the paper towel tube so that the edges can be glued to the sides of the tube.

2. Have your child glue one circle to one end of the paper towel tube. Let the glue dry.

3. Ask your child to crumple aluminum foil into a long thin piece and put it inside the paper towel tube. This will help slow the movement of the pebbles, shells, and so on.

4. Have your child pour the small found objects into the tube.

5. Have them glue the other circle to the other end of the paper towel tube so that both ends are closed.

6. Let your child decorate their nature stick with crayons, markers, and so on.

7. Have your child shake the nature stick to make their own joyful noise!

NATURE BAND

The Jackson 5, Arcade Fire, Kings of Leon, the Jonas Brothers, and other family bands have graced us with their music over the years. Go outside with your child to join their ranks and turn your friends or family into a band for the ages.

 EASY

What You'll Need

Open space

Rocks

Sticks

Multiple players

1. Ask your child about their favorite songs. Ask any other family members or friends who are interested in playing, too, and form a band. (Adults can weigh in on their favorite types of music.)

2. Let your child decide which kind of music they like best and help them choose the music style your band will perform.

3. Tell each member of the band to find sticks and rocks for an instrument.

4. Together, arrange the "instruments" outside in a performance area.

5. Play everyone's favorite songs and rock the night away.

BAT AND MOTH

Bats are extraordinary creatures that employ echolocation—using sound when seeing is not an option—to get around and locate their food. To some, their noises sound like musical notes. Have your child replicate these shrieks and squeaks by playing an exciting and unusual game of tag.

 MEDIUM

What You'll Need

Open space

Cones

A blindfold

Two players (or more)

1. Create a boundary with cones in an open outdoor space. Make sure there are no obstacles in the play area.

2. Blindfold your child and place them in the center of the play area. They are the bat.

3. The other player (the moth) stands still in the play area and claps once.

4. The bat points to where they think the clap came from.

5. The bat is the tagger and the runner is the moth.

6. The bat starts the game by shrieking. Every time the bat shrieks the moth responds with a squeak.

7. Staying within the boundaries, the blindfolded bat tries to tag the moth by finding them with sound alone. (The moth will warn the bat if they get close to leaving the play area.)

8. Once the moth is caught, the bat and moth switch places.

9. Extra players can stand around the edge of the play area, helping the bat and moth stay within the boundaries. For an extra challenge, they become "trees" in the play space, standing still and making a sound whenever the bat gets close to them. Players will take turns being the bat, the moth, and the trees.

TREE BARK GUIRO

A guiro is a ribbed gourd with an opening on one end. It is a percussion instrument that is played by rubbing a stick over the ribs of the gourd. Have your child create a simplified version that helps with the development of hand-eye coordination.

EASY

What You'll Need

Pieces of textured tree bark

A stick a little longer than a pen

1. Together, find pieces of bark (both on trees and off) that your child can use for their instrument and a stick that is slightly thicker and longer than a pen to play the guiro.

2. Have your child look at the texture of the bark and guess which type will make the best sound.

3. Ask your child to run the stick along the bark, listening to the sound it makes. Does the bark sound best when it is on the tree or off? What kind of sound does it make?

BONUS ACTIVITY!

Ask your child to find something red in nature—a leaf, a flower, and so on. Then ask them to make the sound they think the color red would make. Repeat for different colors.

JUST DIDGERIDOO IT

A didgeridoo is a wind instrument originally played in northern Australia thousands of years ago. It's also a fun instrument to make and play. Help your child bring Australia home by creating their very own didgeridoo. Since these instruments can be heard from miles away, bring the whole project outside to see how loud they can make their didgeridoo.

 MEDIUM

What You'll Need

Multiple cardboard tubes (from paper towels, aluminum foil, or toilet paper) of the same width

Glue

Crayons, colored pencils, pens, or markers

1. Have your child line up the cardboard rolls from end to end and glue the ends of the tubes together.

2. Once the glue has dried, let your child decorate the didgeridoo.

3. Once everything has dried, have your child lift one end of the instrument to their mouth and play it.

4. Let your child know that playing a didgeridoo is about releasing controlled breaths. Have them vibrate their lips against the cardboard to create a deep sound.

LANGUAGE OF DRUMS

Your child won't remember a time before technology allowed us to communicate with others all over the world. But in the olden days we had to come up with ways to communicate with those far away. One of those ways was with drums. Help your child communicate with their family through percussion.

 MEDIUM

What You'll Need

Several flat surfaces outside to use as drums (like rocks, the ground, a tree, and so on)

1. Ask your child what they want to say to their family. (Make sure it's a simple word or phrase.)

2. Together, come up with a specific beat for each word or phrase.

3. Practice those beats with one another on your child's first "drum."

4. Move to a new location with a different "drum."

5. Practice the same beats on a different surface. Do they sound the same or different? Can you still understand one another?

9

Calm, Cool, and Collected

The world moves fast; spinning through space at a thousand miles an hour can sometimes seem like the world is spinning out of control. But nature helps us feel grounded. After a busy day together, both parents and children can tap into nature for calming practices. And instilling a sense of calm in the outdoors at a young age can help children develop the tools they can use throughout their lives to deal with stress. Here are activities for mindfulness, meditation, and calm.

SIT SPOT

Finding a way to ground yourself can be difficult. Picking a spot to go back to at a time of stress can help your child work through the things life might throw at them. It will work for you, too!

EASY

What You'll Need

A nearby outdoor area that is both accessible and comfortable

Paper

Pen or pencil

1. Work together to create a list of the feelings that your child experiences. Do they get sad? Or angry?

2. Create a different list of what kind of support your child needs when they feel sad or angry or unhappy. Do they like other people to leave them alone? Do they need to talk about their feelings?

3. Find a spot outdoors where your child can go with you when things get stressful or over-whelming. This spot should be comfortable and easily accessible.

4. Sit down in the spot together and talk about why it is calming and when it would be helpful to go to this space.

BONUS ACTIVITY!

Sit with your child outside and look around for a few minutes. Tell your child to close their eyes and have them list all the objects and animals they remember seeing. Try this as a calming activity.

STORYTELLING

Humans have a rich history of storytelling. And we have always loved origin stories, the stories of how the world came into being: how the bear lost its tail, how islands were made, how the night sky and the stars came to be. Let your child create their own origin story to help them better understand the world around them.

 EASY

What You'll Need

Outdoor space, ideally surrounded by trees and other objects in nature

1. Sit outside with your child in a comfortable space.

2. Ask your child to look at nature and name an object around which they can create an origin story.

3. Help your child come up with their origin story.

   * *Did that object always look like that?*
   * *Did it start out as another object?*
   * *Did it interact with other parts of nature on its way to its current state?*

CLOUD WATCHING

Clouds can ignite your child's imagination. They can see castles, animals, and even themselves in the sky. No matter what shape they take, clouds can calm and soothe and provide a meditative space. What does your child see when they look up into the sky?

 EASY

What You'll Need

A quiet outdoor space

Towels or mats

1. On a partly cloudy day, lay your towels or mats in a quiet, comfortable space outdoors, lie on your back with your child, and look up at the sky.

2. Ask your child to point out a few clouds that interest them. Have them talk about what they see.

3. Tell each other a calming story about the clouds your child has chosen.

BONUS ACTIVITY!

Have your child count the number of clouds that go by. How many can they see in five minutes? How many in 10?

NAPS IN A NEST

Adults love naps. Kids often resist them. Sometimes the best way to help children enjoy something more involves a change of scenery and scenario. Creating a place for a doll, stuffed animal, or action figure to take a nap outdoors helps kids develop a sense of comfort outside and get excited about the idea of nap time.

 EASY

What You'll Need

Sticks, rocks, leaves, or other objects in nature

A doll, stuffed animal, or action figure

1. Work together to find a quiet napping spot.

2. Have your child make a nest for their favorite doll, stuffed animal, or action figure to sleep in. The nest can be a circle of sticks, rocks, leaves, or any other found objects.

3. Ask your child to make the nest as comfortable as possible for a nap.

4. Help your child tell a nature bedtime story as they put their pretend little one to sleep.

FOREST BATHING

For centuries, humans have had a deep connection with nature and its calming abilities. In Japan, forest bathing has been practiced for years. The process involves drinking in the forest using all five of your senses. Just as you would sink into a relaxing bath, you relax into the forest. Doing this with your child teaches them to relax and develop mindfulness meditation skills they can take with them throughout their life.

EASY

What You'll Need

Outdoor space, preferably with trees and other objects in nature

1. Turn off your phone and go for a meandering walk with your child.

2. Together, sit or lie down in a clearing.

3. Listen to the sounds around you. Ask your child what they hear.

4. Look at the objects around you with your child. Have them list what they see.

5. Feel the ground underneath you and the air on your skin. Ask your child to describe what they touch and what touches them.

6. Smell the scents floating around you. Ask your child what they smell. Do they smell different scents from those in your home?

7. Ask your child to imagine what an object they see (like a flower) would taste like.

8. Let nature wash over both of you.

BIRDS FLYING HIGH

We hear birds all the time. Sometimes they can be so loud they wake us up. But how many of them do you and your child see on a daily basis?

EASY

What You'll Need

Outdoor space

1. Let your child choose a comfortable space to sit outside.

2. Look up to the sky together and have your child count all the birds they can see.

3. Ask them to count the birds by color. How many birds with blue feathers do they see? Black feathers? Different-colored feathers?

BONUS ACTIVITY!

Cut a triangle out of cardboard and give it to your child outside. Ask them to find that shape in nature. Try a square and a circle another day. Let them take their time as they search for their shapes.

THE SCENT OF THE AIR

The world is full of scents: the smell of flowers, wet leaves, the ocean, and more. Some of these scents recall memories and others instill new ones. Talk about what the scents mean to your child.

 EASY

What You'll Need

Outdoor space

Paper

Crayons, colored pencils, pens, or markers

1. Walk around outside together and smell the air.

2. Have your child draw what they smell. Is it a flower? A tree? An animal?

3. Ask them what that particular scent reminds them of or makes them think about.

OUTDOOR SCHOOL

Danish schools often hold classes outdoors to foster connections between schools, nature, and communities. Outdoor school, or *udeskole*, has resulted in a higher level of well-being for students. Which activities would your child like to move from inside to outside?

 MEDIUM

What You'll Need

Outdoor space

1. Ask your child about the different parts of their life. What do they do every day? Eat meals? Play? Watch TV?

2. Talk about which activities they would like to do outside.

3. Come up with a plan together to move at least one of those activities outdoors. How soon can you do it?

INSIDE, OUTSIDE SOUNDS

There are so many sounds inside and outside that sometimes we don't hear all of them. By listening carefully your child can list what they hear—and what they *don't* hear. Try this meditative activity with your child for a calming experience.

EASY

What You'll Need

Outdoor space

Paper

Pen or pencil

1. Sitting inside with your child, list the sounds you each hear in your home.

2. Head outside and list the sounds you each hear in nature.

3. Help your child circle the sounds you both like on the indoor list that you wish were on the outdoor list and the sounds you both like on the outdoor list that you wish were on the indoor list.

4. Ask them to draw a line between the sounds that are on both lists.

5. Have them draw a star next to the sounds that they like to hear and make them feel calm.

THE STORY OF STARS

When night falls, the stars come out. For thousands of years, people have used the stars to create stories that explain the world. Help your child create their own constellation and write a story about it.

 MEDIUM

What You'll Need

Outdoor space at nightfall or a picture of the night sky

Paper

Pen or pencil

1. Take your child outside at night to look at the stars. (If darkness falls too late at night, show them a picture of the night sky.) Talk about how they can see people and animals in the star patterns and how the constellations have stories behind them.

2. Ask your child to draw a picture of their own constellation. They can draw a person (a family member, a teacher, a neighbor) or an animal (a wild animal, a pet, a farm animal).

3. Ask them to tell the story about the constellation. How did that person or animal end up among the stars? Write down their story for posterity.

SLEEPING LIONS

Even being quiet can become competitive. Turn being the quietest and the calmest into a sport that allows your child to slow down and think about what is around them.

EASY

What You'll Need

Outdoor space
to lie down

Towels or mats

Multiple players

1. Ask your child to find a comfortable spot outdoors where they would like to lie down.

2. Place the towels or mats on that spot.

3. Have everyone lie down and get their giggles and wiggles out.

4. Once everyone is calm, one player states that the game will start.

5. Once the game has started, no one can move. Whoever moves or makes a sound is out. The last one to move or make a sound is the winner.

6. Ask everyone what they were thinking about in the quiet: Were they thinking about the birds overhead? The worms under the ground? The wind blowing through the trees?

ALPHABETICAL WORLD

Help your child learn the alphabet mindfully by sitting quietly and calling out what they can see or sense that starts with every letter of the alphabet.

CHALLENGING

What You'll Need

Outdoor space

1. Find a comfortable space to sit.

2. Sing the alphabet together out loud.

3. Beginning with *A*, have your child name what they can see that starts with each letter of the alphabet. (They can also list things they sense but can't see—like air or bugs that may be underground.) Feel free to skip letters that are impossible to find or make up a new word for that letter.

4. Once you have worked your way through the alphabet, sing the alphabet song again, pointing to the objects your child has identified for each letter.

Resources

Gray, Peter. *Free to Learn: Why Unleashing the Instinct to Play Will Make Our Children Happier, More Self-Reliant, and Better Students for Life.*

Hanscom, Angela J. *Balanced and Barefoot: How Unrestricted Outdoor Play Makes for Strong, Confident, and Capable Children.*

Louv, Richard. *Last Child in the Woods: Saving Our Children from Nature-Deficit Disorder.*

McGurk, Linda Åkeson. *There's No Such Thing as Bad Weather: A Scandinavian Mom's Secrets for Raising Healthy, Resilient, and Confident Kids.*

Sampson, Scott D. *How to Raise a Wild Child: The Art and Science of Falling in Love with Nature.*

Singer, Marilyn. *A Stick Is an Excellent Thing: Poems Celebrating Outdoor Play.*

Acknowledgments

No journey is just one foot in front of the other. There are the moments when you get lost, when you trip over your own feet and cannot find the trail markers. None of us walks a path alone. We have help along the way. I would like to thank those whose paths crossed mine and who gave me a hand when they could.

Like Susan, who put this idea together and then somehow did not call me every day in sheer perplexity over what I had written on the page, and instead was kind, excited, and patient.

I would like to thank my parents, who will come and find me no matter how many times my car breaks down. They encourage me to see what is out there while always welcoming me home.

Nothing would be complete without thanking my brothers, who are somehow still around and pick up when I call.

But this book would not have been made if it were not for those who walked with me on my journey in the outdoors, those who opened their arms and hearts and answered every question I could ever have about gear and knots. Thank you to Zachary and Brendan, who encouraged me and became my brothers when I knew nothing. Thank you to all who have ever lived at Lane (including Mckenna and Stevo), those who lived there before me for setting things into place and showing nothing but support and kindness, and those who lived at Lane with me. Through the ups and downs, the moments of stress and laughs, you taught me more about myself and the outdoors in one year than I thought possible, and I thank you. Thank you to Cody, who has lived in some of the strangest situations with me and yet keeps hanging out with me, and Kayleigh, who has the patience and empathy of a saint. I ask myself what you would do in at least one situation a day. Thank you to those who I did not name but still hold all the love and respect for—those who taught me everything about this big crazy world and the outdoor industry.

Index

About the Author

Samantha Lewis has worked in outdoor education since 2015 in New Zealand, Colorado, China, and Massachusetts. She was most recently a lead preschool teacher at an outdoor preschool in Massachusetts. Samantha lives in New England, where she loves to hear the crunch of leaves in the fall, go skiing in the winter, smell the flowers in the spring, and swim in the ocean during the summer. But mostly she is always up for a new adventure.

From board books to reads for teens, **Brightly** helps raise lifelong readers by celebrating the countless adventures and moments of connection that books can offer. We take pride in working with a diverse group of contributors, authors, and partners who provide a multitude of ways to cultivate a love of books and reading in children of all ages.

Thank you for coming on this adventure with us! A Brightly Book is expertly designed to provide young readers with a fun, age-appropriate, and hands-on learning experience. We hope you and your little ones enjoy this book as much as we do.

Happy Reading!

See all that Brightly has to offer at **readbrightly.com.**